PEARL & APHORISMS FROM THE EROTIC POLITICIAN

ISBN 978-1-300-88377-7

This book is dedicated to Gordon Pearson. He never turned away.

CHARACTERS

ANNA – Daughter of Paul

ARIEL – Daughter of Richard

CLAUDIUS – Torturer

DAVID – Poet

JACK – Fool

JULIA – Daughter of Richard

KATHARINE – Queen

PAUL – Revolutionary

PEARL – Slave to Richard

PIERCE – Steward

RICHARD – King

ROYAL GUARDSMEN

VICTOR – Prince

ACT I SCENE 1

(Pierce stands before his enthroned King.)

PIERCE - I am fresh from rounds of torture my lord. What is your need?

RICHARD - What a grand inquisitor you would have been. Feeding on fear has made you strong. Some are born for the whip. Your mastery of the weapon enthralls me. I salivate watching you strip men of skin, women of beauty, and mothers of hope.

PIERCE - I'll die an evil man. The Crown's enchantment cannot be broken, nor would I desire release from it. Veins of precious metal open at your command. Wealth flows into the war chest and adorns the bodies of your servants. They shine beside statues they bring to life. These tyrants, most worthy of emulation, inspire cruelty. Their pitiless gaze does not allow weakness in this castle! Bejeweled women, inflamed, crawl toward your throne. Flesh is offered for your amusement and bleeds for your pleasure. The Crown is symbol of all I adore.

RICHARD - Darkness has swallowed my seed of eternity.

PIERCE - I have summoned Victor.

RICHARD - Excellent.

(Enter Victor.)

VICTOR - My lord, how will I serve you?

RICHARD - Someone has stolen my Pearl. What fool did this?

(Jack enters.)

VICTOR - A man in love.

JACK - I do not love.

VICTOR - Have you seen the way our poet looks at Pearl?

JACK - Shove him back in his clam!

PIERCE - Love is repulsive. His writing has lost vigor.

JACK - A malady that devours heart and mind. Your caged organ is safe brother - you have no mind to conceive the abstraction.

(Jack leaves stage.)

RICHARD - Heir to the throne, will you endure your mother's venom? Sleepless victims suffer hallucinations of the damned. Her lust drives them hard and deep into nightmare.

VICTOR - I am steeped in the blood of her cruelty and the glory of your reign is my constant study.

RICHARD - The crown is heavy. You must walk through walls of screaming fire, swim through rivers of blood, and be consort of Death.

VICTOR - I have the strength to rule. Pearl will be found.

(Exit Victor.)

PIERCE - If he fails?

RICHARD - I'll crucify women upside down and nail their children above them. Chained men will encircle wives and offspring in a ring of fire. Neighboring states shall be forced into battle. My soldiers will hack through forests of men, limbs will cover blood soaked earth, heads on pikes will jut from the hot, seeping, wound.

PIERCE - Desire for war distills my rage.

RICHARD - Wound together, a whip of lightning, we enrapture this world!

SCENE 2

(Pearl and David in his study.)

PEARL - There's no escaping Richard. You'll die if I stay.

DAVID - I only fear life without you.

PEARL - Forget about me. Continue writing for the Crown. Use the gift of language to gain wealth and immortality.

DAVID - Only the present matters! Live with me in open defiance of Richard, die in my arms, inspire the mob to burn the royal family alive in their castle!

PEARL - Live for your art, enchant people, show them beauty is not dead.

DAVID - Kneel, watch King Richard lick your halo with his tongue of fire? My poems will be shadows of desire.

PEARL - Richard owns me. He claims paternity and obsessively retells the story of my creation - I was a spark in his mind which he encased in semen: his consciousness fleshed out my body.

DAVID - The King gave me a beautiful knife with an ivory handle. We'll suicide ourselves. While he rages below, ripping apart our bodies, we'll merge and vibrate in harmony with the music of the spheres.

PEARL - Richard will send his prince of Hell. Victor hunts humans for sport. He's been running them down since he learned how to ride. I screamed while he beat my father to the ground, stabbed him, and raped my mother in the spreading pool of blood.

DAVID - Life is a curse! I no longer recognize the sovereignty of Richard and his brood. Fear of pain keeps the populace enslaved! Last year I was feasting with friends. My songs are nothing compared to the poetry lived by the man and his wife. Their children were radiant. Animals felt the sweetness of their love as it spread with sunlight over the forest surrounding their cottage. A week before dinner, at the market, a soldier stood beside me as John spoke against his monarch. “A strong king eases the burden of his subjects. Life is meant to be enjoyed. Happiness should be expanded till all know their true value. What a kingdom we could have if love flowed from the Crown into every hearth.” Sarah was serving sweets when a soldier kicked open the door.

PEARL - What happened to those beautiful people?

DAVID - I don’t want to know.

(Victor enters with Royal Guardsmen.)

VICTOR - Take Pearl.

(Royal Guardsmen tear her away from David. She is taken offstage and David is forced to his knees. Victor grabs his throat.)

In time you’ll see the wisdom of your father’s decision. He is working to save you from the disease of love. Many good men have been lost to the affliction. Strength of mind is lost when the parasite takes root in the heart.

DAVID - He is not my father!

(Victor clamps hand over David’s mouth.)

VICTOR - He’s father to everyone in this kingdom. His right to the flesh of subjects is indisputable.

(Hand from David’s mouth removed.)

DAVID - Bring me before the King! The charge against love must be refuted.

VICTOR - Lust will burn love from your heart. Only then will you be worthy of kneeling before the Crown. We will puncture the precious fruit of families on our journey to the castle and you will become inebriated by the constant flow of nectar.

SCENE 3

(King and Queen enthroned at court. David, Pearl, Pierce, and Victor are before them. Royal Guardsmen hold arms of David.)

RICHARD - Well done Victor.

VICTOR - Serving the Crown is my pleasure.

RICHARD - David does not share your enthusiasm.

DAVID - Harness the beasts you claim as family before all good feeling is destroyed in you.

RICHARD - Think of the masterworks you created under my influence. Fantasies flowed from your black pen and bled through your white sheets into the dreaming body of the populace. When you sang of my sensual cruelty in love and war I showered you with gold coins and precious stones.

(Jack comes from behind King's throne. Walks with cane.)

DAVID - You are lost without love.

RICHARD - Absurd.

JACK - You define reality.

DAVID - You are beneath the woman you have enslaved. We are in sacred union.

JACK - The slave who was beneath you is now with her master.

(Pokes David in belly with cane, then walks over to Pearl. King explodes with laughter.)

RICHARD - Katharine! Sink your claws into soft David. Or should I give him to Claudius?

PEARL - Neither! It will cost you nothing to free us!

(Jack pulls dagger from cane and holds it against Pearl's throat.)

JACK - Your lips, above and below, are his to chew. He will bite, suck, and tear your breasts when it pleases him. Blood from your ravishing body inspires war.

(Pearl shuddering and crying.)

PEARL - No no no.

RICHARD - Claudius!

(Claudius enters dressed as executioner: black hood, shirtless, black pants, and black boots. Jack steps away from Pearl. Claudius throws her over shoulder and walks offstage. Jack puts dagger back in cane and follows.)

DAVID - Take another to inspire war. I will continue to rhapsodize your history in exchange for Pearl.

(Katharine steps down from throne and walks to David.)

KATHARINE - Do as we command slave. When emotions spill over I drink them down. You are a goblet encrusted with blood and tears.

DAVID - Whore!

KATHARINE - Yes! Blades and whips will release your liquor.

VICTOR - Embrace your Queen David. Ecstatic devotees swallow sacraments secreted from her body. After communion, anointed limbs lock on the temple floor and tangle into a writhing wreath.

(Royal Guardsman enters.)

ROYAL GUARDSMAN - King, there is an uprising. A man named Paul is exciting the people to revolt. He paints you as selfish and depraved. He shouts in the streets that only your demise can bring freedom and happiness.

RICHARD - Preposterous!

PIERCE - Force them to swallow steel. Cruelty is the pleasure of the strong.

(Laughter erupts from Richard.)

Victor, capture Paul and his pretty niece. He loves her above all things. Transforming our kingdom into an engine of war will be far easier if we pervert him. The Crown must bind all flesh.

RICHARD - Your tongue is a blade. How easily you slice away superfluities. Force the proud man into the flesh of his niece. Lust will ignite him and with us he'll devour enemies and enslave the world.

(All leave but King and Queen.)

KATHARINE - I'll squeeze the poison from his cock. Love will not claim him.

(Darkness.)

SCENE 4

(Pierce and Paul in court. Paul held by two Royal Guardsmen.)

PAUL - You are not men!

PIERCE - We are vessels overflowing with the passions of power.

PAUL - Inebriation will give way to madness.

PIERCE - What is more pleasurable than the euphoria of evil? Amplify desires beyond human measure. Learn from me secrets of union with the Dark Goddess.

PAUL - You are perverted beyond redemption and have made the royal children worthless. Salvation is lost.

PIERCE - Salvation is the dream of weaklings. Pluck roses and shred them for pleasure.

PAUL - I have no taste for sin. A body is not to be displayed as trophy, abused for sport, or forced into labor to further enrich besotted aristocrats. Life is a precious gift. Spent wisely, in pursuit of pure knowledge, lasting happiness is found and shared.

PIERCE - What piss! Human flesh fills my belly. Skin from victims covers books I read about great men and war. I drink blood from skulls and become drunk on fear and hate. Women slave under the blazing sun of my lust – they water their mutilated flowers with tears.

PAUL - Lives you ruin populate the hell you make for yourself.

PIERCE - Bodies exist for my pleasure. I have someone for you to terrorize.

PAUL - You are foul.

PIERCE - Feed with me on her anguished flesh.

(Claudius brings in Paul’s niece. Anna is gagged.)

PAUL - Anna!

PIERCE - She writhes for us.

PAUL - Damn you!

PIERCE - Tear open this sweet fruit. Turn away from disrupting subjects of the Crown. Monarchy is the burden beasts must bear.

PAUL - Diseased pig! Release her!

PIERCE - Brutalize her with power!

(Paul lunges at Pierce and is pulled back by Royal Guardsmen. Claudius grips Anna's throat.)

PAUL - How can you exist, estranged from all things good and beautiful?

PIERCE - I will feast on the flesh of your niece with the royal family.

(Pierce stabs Paul in belly. Queen arrives in chariot pulled by two women.)

KATHARINE - Perfect timing! A fresh kill!

PIERCE - You should have witnessed the foreplay.

KATHARINE - Flames lick my thighs.

(Steps from chariot and walks to Anna. Grabs hair and licks tears from cheeks.)

Delicious child, after an evening with me you'll beg for Death.

(Darkness.)

ACT II SCENE 1

(Pierce addresses audience as citizens of the Crown.)

PIERCE - Citizens, Paul has been executed for crimes against the Crown. He wanted your strength to throw down the Royal Family, wanted to take by force what is theirs by right of birth. The power he craved would allow him a life of uninterrupted depravity. His niece is under our care. Between sobs, she told us of whippings and perpetual rape during enslavement. We share your outrage.

(Darkness.)

SCENE 2

(Pierce and Richard sit at a table in Pierce's study. On the table are two glasses and a bottle of liquor.)

RICHARD - Hunger is exacerbated by feeding on what I crave. Swirling my tongue in the Eternal Wound, squeezing blood streaked breasts, binds me tighter to flesh.

PIERCE - The first step of liberation is over a body one has mastered. My first was succulent, like a perfectly ripe peach. I drained her of tears.

RICHARD - My daughters are swollen with pride. Under your tutelage they have become striking creatures. I am pleased you send them into the city to offer their bodies to strangers. Ending those nocturnal rites by slaughtering the men and women they pleasure is genius.

PIERCE - They feast on subjects with animal pleasure. Orgies in the Garden of Red Delights have raised their level of endurance almost to the level of their mother. Remember Katharine's rage when sex frightened them?

(Both laugh lustily.)

RICHARD - How beautifully they flower under her tyranny.

(Richard swallows his drink and leaves. Julia enters and sits down.)

JULIA - My belly swells with life uncle.

PIERCE - Who is the father?

JULIA - You, father, Victor?

PIERCE - What will you name the beast?

JULIA - Pierce. You enrapture me. I demand the same from my son.

PIERCE - If it's a girl?

JULIA - I'll kill her. I want the special relationship only a son and mother can have.

PIERCE - Yes.

JULIA - My breasts are his sun and moon. These eyes you stare into are the night he'll fall into. I'll sit proudly beside him as he grows in stature. In our bed I'll inflame his lust for power. Serpents and swords await the voice of my unborn king. We'll ravage Earth. My son feeds on these thoughts, growing strong in my womb. When he bursts into cold air I'll give him a bloody breast to suck.

PIERCE - Your heart beats an intoxicating rhythm. I thirst for the liquor pumping through your body. Plunging a sword into an enemy is the same as thrusting my cock inside your flesh.

JULIA - When you read me Suetonius before bed I stayed awake as long as I could. The chapter on the reign of Nero was my favorite. His cruelty excited my imagination. I pretended to be the son of Agrippina and Gnaeus. Both filled their roles perfectly. It was all great fun. Father enjoyed playing a character from Rome's glorious past. When he first asked which part of Nero's family history I wished recreated I shouted, "Gnaeus running over a boy with his chariot!" What a thrill to see the speed of the conveyance increase as the lad was thrown onto the street. At night I held the image of the small, broken, body in my mind. What warm, sweet, tears I tasted as I drifted into sleep.

PIERCE - I've a bust of Nero in my bedchamber. The relationship he had with his mother inspires my debauches. The other night I sprung from a cage wearing a lion skin, attacked bodies bound to trees in the Garden of Red Delights, and held jewels from mutilated genitalia in my mouth.

JULIA - My birthday! Remember the evening of my twelfth birthday? You stood aloof in your chariot, encircled by beautiful creatures. The crucified, selected for the occasion with great care, roared in the fire devouring them.

(Julia kisses Pierce, long and slow on the mouth, then exits.)

PIERCE - Women. I slide through red velvet hell enraged. Pleasure deforms and destroys. I must continuously outrage the entrance to my former paradise.

(Ariel enters.)

ARIEL - Whore! Whore! Whore! they shouted as I walked through the market. I should have ordered a guardsman to nail me on the spot. Yes! After killing a woman! He and the others might still be hammering me into her flesh.

PIERCE - Spectacle, the intimacy of violence, binds subjects to superiors.

ARIEL - The fantasy consumes me.

PIERCE - As you grind out orgasms I will whip screams from victims till they collapse.

ARIEL - I'll rub myself raw.

PIERCE - Stroke on this - pain flows from the Dark Queen, through our bodies, into victims we select for Her pleasure. Amplified pain surges back into Her: the nexus of the web spasms. Insatiable appetite demands highly skilled technicians of pleasure. The raw delights we consume sustain the ecstasy of Mother.

ARIEL - My womb shall be ready for the new creatures when the violence of the orgy destroys my individuality. They will rip from my belly, drink hot blood, and devour my heart. The future is red!

PIERCE - Hecate will feast with your offspring on your sweet flesh.

ARIEL - Lust for her is like being ravished by fire. Fear is taking hold of me.

PIERCE - Why fear being consumed by your strongest desire?

ARIEL - If madness quickly follows how will I endure it?

PIERCE - Madness is a transitional state. Boldly traverse the realm. Execute your desires with precision upon your return.

ARIEL - Guide me.

PIERCE - We all find our own way.

SCENE 3

(King, Queen, Ariel, Claudius, Julia, and Pierce lounge on couches. Anna, leashed and gagged, is on her knees beside Claudius.)

RICHARD - Claudius, did your bitch enjoy the Garden of Red Delights?

CLAUDIUS - Screamed till she passed out. Shrieked when she awakened, so I gagged her.

KATHARINE - I salivate. Her young flesh will slide down my throat. The horror swelling her eyes tickles my belly. How easily I could suck her organs of sight into my mouth and grind them to nothing.

PIERCE - After ravishing Anna we'll feast on some rare creatures I've procured - girls, with crab-like exoskeletons over their cunts. Cracking, splitting, and tearing those shells will give our feast an intimacy lacking outside our circle of libertinism. Twisting my fork in their soft flesh will exceed all previous pleasures.

(Ariel draped lasciviously over Julia.)

ARIEL - Anna weeps! She must cry over the cunts we shred.

JULIA - Yum! I salivate in anticipation of our succulent spread.

ARIEL - Oral delirium.

RICHARD - We are enthralled.

PIERCE - Mutilated flowers are my fetish. I divine the future by reading disfiguration.

KATHARINE - I will bite their lips and swallow sweet, red, pain.

JULIA - Pierce! A show after the feast!

PIERCE - What is your pleasure?

JULIA - To share my playthings. I've been starving them in anticipation of such a glorious evening. Claudius can drill diamond teeth into their gums.

KATHARINE - Marvelous!

(Ariel crawls over to Queen and mounts her.)

ARIEL - I seek to become as grand and pitiless as you mother. Voluptuous cruelty transformed you into a sexual predator. Make my body a quaking, bleeding, altar on which humans are sacrificed. Use me to explore the depths of perversion. When I emerge, having mastered the disciplines of the damned, I shall carve my name in the black stele of life.

(Julia walks over to Anna, takes leash from Claudius, and molests her while speaking. Claudius leaves stage.)

JULIA - Tyranny over sexual objects unmasks power. Cruelty awakens us to the manifold pleasures of pain. We release dreams imprisoned in flesh.

PIERCE - Conjure Hecate with the violence of your rituals! Become drunk with her on emotions drained from victims. Distill quintessence of agony, hate, and sorrow.

(Claudius returns with two girls held by neck. He shoves them onto floor and Royal Family attacks them. Stage flooded by red light, filled with screaming, and immediately followed by darkness.)

ACT III SCENE 1

(Ariel and Julia walk through Garden of Red Delights. They stop below a crucified woman.)

ARIEL - I miss father's transports of rage.

JULIA - Unrivalled.

ARIEL - He exhausted himself raving about Hecate.

JULIA - Can you still recite his evocation?

ARIEL - Goddess of witches! Teach your satyr spells to conjure pleasure beyond mortal making! I tear breasts of nymphs with claws and teeth and rip out hearts for your pleasure. Hot blood flows continuously to inebriate you Hecate! Each soul I send is a kiss.

JULIA - My fantasy was to die from his violence.

ARIEL - He favored you.

JULIA - I was proud to be impaled on his horn.

ARIEL - I want his venom inside me.

JULIA - Paul, the pleb, said Pierce suffered from ignorance.

ARIEL - Of what?

JULIA - Love.

ARIEL - The wealth of our kingdom has spun the globe for us. We've experienced the known world with Pierce. He has forced from our flesh the burning truth – love is privation.

JULIA - He prepared us for Mother.

ARIEL - Idealization of strength and beauty, pale altar on which devotees sacrifice themselves night and day. Blood streams from her breasts and belly over shaking legs. What brings more pleasure than Death devouring us?

JULIA - Sexual violence pulls darkness into human form. The way She ravishes Mother unhinges me.

ARIEL - Blades plunge every hour into enslaved hearts. Suicides increase the appetite for slaughter driving her orgies.

(King runs onto stage. He is hysterical.)

RICHARD - Renounce the Crown! I've wasted my life!

JULIA - Father?

RICHARD - Embrace me, I'll soon be killed.

ARIEL - For our pleasure!

RICHARD - Ariel?

ARIEL - Only a beast worthy of my flesh may utter my name.

JULIA - My raw, red, rose burns for you.

RICHARD - Banish those thoughts.

JULIA - I will mount you when you die, and swallow your seed. The creature that crawls from my womb will be made to despise weakness.

(Victor enters. Walks to Father, shakes him roughly, and throws him down.)

VICTOR - This behavior is unworthy of a king! Begging for affection from bodies you own!

ARIEL - Votaries! Show me organs, sliding and swallowing feverishly. Banish all restraint! Convulse yourselves with the pleasure of regicide. I crave the violence of your lust!

(Naked males and females crawl and slide onto stage. They overpower screaming Richard while his offspring ravish each other.)

SCENE 2

(Pearl in middle of dark stage with spotlight on her. Light becomes red during monologue.)

PEARL - Tears burn my lacerated breasts. I'll dig Katharine's eyes from her sockets with my nails and rip the heart from her chest. Enter me Hecate, become inebriated on my hate, give me the strength to kill the Queen, give me her son, her naked power, and I'll be your slave to slowly devour.

(Darkness.)

END

APHORISMS FROM THE EROTIC POLITICIAN

Sex is violence.

Love is the dormant state of lust.

A beautiful woman is the perfection of cruelty.

Erotic politicians exist to enrapture the Sacred Whore.

Tortured devils adore angels of cruelty.

The weak love being whipped by the strong. They are transfigured by the miracle of pain.

Fear is an aphrodisiac.

Revere thyself! Become a fountain of pleasure.

Blood is the liquor we crave.

Those who steep themselves in cruelty emerge with a demonic will. They whip with lightning.

Heaven is power. Weakness is Hell.

Orgasm is plenitude. Evil forces the white hot crown upon the rose.

I seed the altar of flesh and bleed the mystery of Woman.

Freedom is fiction. All flesh is bound by the desire to rule or be ruled.

Death is not the limit of sexual expression.

Seductive language of the Sacred Whore entangles seekers of Truth in the barbed wire of hidden desire.

The Serpent flicks the fruit of Good and Evil between female thighs.

Take root in the organ of love. Feed on lust and despair.

Bodies are generated and enraptured by solar incest.

Suffering binds human animals to the Sacred Whore. Blood is thick on the chain driving diabolical history.

Victims ascend in value as anguish increases.

Hate is preached in a forest of bodies ablaze. Slavering beasts break bones and feast in the widening circle of power. Angels are inebriated by the spectacle.

Murder is the apex of life. Slayer and slain are united in the ecstasy of violence.

The merciless torture themselves with introspection.

Semen of serpentine peers transfigure this world. Offspring exist entirely for the pleasure of the Sacred Whore. Discharge of eroticized pain illuminates her crown.

Eyes roll back in skulls of the damned as names are struck from the scrolls of Heaven.

Horned beasts discourse in opulent courts, decide the ruin of nations, spin theories of science, literature, and law: a right is a privilege granted by the strong.

Democracy is a perversion of government. Subjecting a nation to the will of the people outrages nature and retards spiritual evolution.

Woman is entirely flesh: bred for pleasure, born in harness, and bleeding for life. The source of her pleasure is pain.

Only children and historians are haunted by the fading ghost of democracy.

A sister planted her infant sibling and watered her daily to watch her grow. She was puzzled after the soft head rotted and ripped it from black earth. Memory of her sister faded as the corpse rapidly decomposed.

Mutilated flowers undulate under the red blade of the harlequin. Wine spills from his mouth and skin. Members of court swarm his twitching body. Participation in State ritual is compulsory.

Claws of Adepts trace lips, areolas, and navels of swollen bellies on black altars. Foreplay augments lust for sacrifice.

A lewd creature was bled white during the Saturnalia. Before losing consciousness I tasted tears and bit into pink, hot, succulent cheeks. The beauty of her sadness poeticized my existence.

An imbecile sat smiling in a stall. His father sent in a prostitute to make him a man. An hour later, he walked into the barn to congratulate his son. The woman was face down on the straw covered earth. The patriarch gripped her long, thick, red braid and pulled up the head to look into her green eyes. Slowly, the soft rope slid through his hand. He squeezed the back of his son's neck, praised him, then kicked apart the legs of the whore. He unbuckled his black leather belt and crawled over the corpse. Reason had overcome passion.

Honey blonde hair spread over my shoulders. Beautiful blue eyes filled with perversion and hatred. I could not hold the gaze of the angel and spiraled upward on the coils of the red serpent toward succulent apples of gold.

Why wouldn't Nero have suicided Seneca? We now revere the corpulent stoic.

Testicles bulge from the eye sockets of a besotted aristocrat. Intestines burst from his skull and sulci drip blood from the throbbing brain below his cock. The pain during his previous incarnation as emperor was excruciating.

Predators learn the art of seduction behind serene masks. Masterpieces are crafted from human remains. Below skeletal hands, at the base of spinal columns, fetishists extract organs in surgical theaters. Brains are scooped from skulls and ooze secrets in silver bowls. Entrails slither over pale thighs into the Eternal Wound.

My catechism was terminated when mother learned the wife of the instructor smashed his head with a hammer. His ecstasy had overwhelmed her. I imagine her weeping, on her knees, at the mercy of her inquisitor.

Is Death the greatest evil? Slaves stretch her demonhole. Transfiguration is instantaneous. Squealing hogs slide into the red, gaping, pit.

Contagion spread quickly through the asylum. Slick pink bodies reek of shit. Black hooves clack through pools of blood spreading over concrete floors. A stone bust of Jung is in the center of each circular cell. Ancestral masks and red handprints encircle the fetish. Inmates within the dream are immortal.

Eruptions of laughter overwhelmed the psychoanalyst. His obsession melted the eyes of men with hot coals. Milk streamed from her breasts into their mouths. Labor will be induced, while they scream, to force from her womb an abomination conceived in the abstract.

She swallowed the yam with her ass. Whispered words of power thickened the root. The Fallen chortled as sweet flesh roasted inside her. Emerald doors to the Palace of Light closed slowly. Weeping, raw from birthing the nightmare root, Celeste no longer heard the music of the spheres. Soft hands burned and brains were seared. Sealed inside was the image of the screeching fetish. A ring of red robed spectators stroked themselves to orgasm in the screen memory.

Delusional from the dark root, she begged for salvation and streamed tears for hallucinated beings of light. Essence of anguish shimmered on flesh she had mutilated with her teeth. From behind her slid a sibling with honey-blonde hair. She devoured the succulent remains then conversed with angels ignoring her sister. Celeste knew her fate when they began to laugh.

Creatures of astonishing beauty, perfected by hate, are one breath from the Divine.

Heavenly creatures are coveted by the damned. Torment of unrequited love disfigures the finest specimens.

Seraphim sing in pyramids capped with gold. Serpents spiral upward and downward spines of devotees. Children of God join the chorus as disciples of darkness vanish. Which is the more ecstatic union?

A lewd sermon was given - delicious, unexpected, absurd. Smoke rose from the lectern of marble and gold. Flames leapt from the pages of the Bible. Fire devoured the preacher as he cursed the congregation. Money spilled from baskets still being stuffed were passed through pews inlaid with silver. Serene Sisters, exquisitely beautiful, levitated below saints on stained glass. They smiled, lids half-closed, eyes unblinking, as the blasphemer roasted.

Envenomed, whispering, my bride suffocated a stranger between her thighs. Both were silent after the catechist inscribed her name on my heart. Salvation is the dream of a child.

Lovers curse my wife. They are appalled by my devotion to the creature with large green eyes and long red hair. Within baroque symbols, with ancient tongues, they chant sadistic spells. The violence they do themselves causes my consort great anguish. Blood drips from the Crown of our union.

A wicked grin stretched the face of my nemesis into a mask of perverted beauty. Stitches pulled from raw wounds thread the spine of the document in which our lethal alliance is enshrined. Extravagant language inebriates while confounding the self-lacerating body-politic.

The argument for equality died on surveillance screens.

A dark fool has procured a succulent object for his queen. Eye contact is made, pain extraction begins, and claws of the matriarch tear the slave's demon-hole. Inside they slide and shred velvet. Laughter erupts from the harlequin as the feast begins.

A blade pierced the organ of love in the labyrinth of mind. The murderer was lost in murmuring darkness.

Cruel Death, fate of all flesh, masks her beauty for the blessed.

After invasive therapy I stripped naked and ran into the woods for my first kill. Strangling the girl with my bare hands, bleeding her in moonlight, enraptured me. I became protégé to the pain technician I worship. Slowly, by slavish devotion, I extract a secret forbidden to articulate.

Blood streaks from a fresh pair of eyes over glass. The skull is magnificent on my black desk. Slowly, the patient sinks into my thought stream. Below the surface she babbles memories from my childhood. Translucent, bleeding, breasts disrupt the fantasy.

Madness has been induced. Patients encircle the contortionist and disrobe in red light. Wondrous productions abound in the state funded asylum. Skin crawls from the cold hands of an angel. She sings to glistening skeletons as she strips skeptics of flesh. The psychoanalyst is rewarded with the knowledge he craves.

The master of the dark art feeds upon ensorcelled slaves. Perfection is achieved when they fall silent, cease blinking, and are motionless.

Aberrations disturb the doctor. A bronze, broken, corpse fades from sight with a smile.

Punch drunk twins arrived in American flag berkas. Red, white, and bruised, bleeding love, they have scheduled a self-immolation. One remains silent and the other sings to the Sacred Whore as they are devoured by fire.

A friend lost an arm. Stumped by the cruelty of the universe, he invited a homeless man to his dachshund's birthday party. The guest informed his host religion was a blight on pornography. Chip growled as phantom pain buckled his master.

A man sketched his daughter in a cell filled with the musky scent of frankincense. He had taken a vow of silence. Words cannot describe the beauty of filming her death.

Porno the Clown is wonderful on the campaign trail. Kids were scattered like broken toys after weddings and funerals. Inseminated newlyweds wept as we waved goodbye. Wives alternated between hysteria and homicidal fantasy as our offspring swelled their wombs.

Celeste joined an execution squad to masturbate over mass graves. Mouths moved slowly in murmuring pits. She stroked herself vigorously as fingers of the dying brushed her inner thighs. A fine example of transactional politics - she eliminates my opponents then lives out her fantasy.

Footage of Celeste's genocidal exploits went viral on social media. Backlash was instant and brutal. Protesters swarmed city streets. Self-harm escalated quickly to suicide. Students from elite universities slashed their throats, hundreds held hands and chanted in walls of fire, screaming clusters fell from planes without parachutes. Those below cheered when abandoned aircraft slammed into skyscrapers, steeples, and exploded. With outstretched arms they welcomed smoking wings, wheels, and sections of fuselage. Ascension was inevitable after my rabid supporters consumed the documentary made from the carnage.

Bittersweet delights are hallucinated in darkness. Viscera slides from splayed hands back into torsos. Flickering tongues slide toward bloody fingertips. Invasive therapy induces transfiguration.

Whores, with solid red eyes, crave excesses of the ancient world. The Colosseum of Rome is reconstructed for their pleasure. Creatures responsible for my elevation execute passions with impunity. Law is the will of serpentine aristocracy.

Introspective sadists are ideal administrators.

Hate blooms in silence, wounds spread over battlefields, angels extract the essence of suffering. Hymns they sing enrage lords of the earth.

The mind of the human animal has been calibrated for atrocity.

Imagination augments cruelty of legislators. Hooves split craniums as they discharge. Succulent sexual organs are ripped from spines and devoured. Lust is the matrix of law.

Skulls of egalitarians have been excavated. Dialogue with peers will no longer suffer interruption.

Life is hallucinated in the realm of Death.

What more devious fiction exists than equality?

Desire for cruelty surges during coercion. Ecstasy of dominion over flesh is the vertex of partisanship.

Inflicting and receiving pain exceeds all other desires. Bruised, torn, blood-streaked flesh is the map of the unconscious.

Dark fools ingurgitate eruptions of laughter. Porcine senators expire from kuru and collapse around a cyclopean statue of Nero. Bloody fingers pluck strings of a lyre. A castrato finds his voice in the Golden House.

Overpopulation is no longer an issue – the finest specimens rip from wombs to feed.

Limbs of succulent longpig fill display cases. Salivating statesmen press hands and lips against glass while bodies are dismembered on stainless steel tables. Coveted organs are extracted, wrapped in butcher paper, and received by the most elevated members of society.

Anna was a lithe creature, with long golden hair and large eyes of solid amber. She spoke only in solitude, for the pleasure of hearing her voice. Transcend terrestrial beauty in silence.

Envenomed clown offspring discharge invective from the bench. Malevolent spirits manifest for the black robed fanatics. Tonsured skulls are split by gavels and slithering intestines spread over the curved ceiling. Journalists carve odious, ancient, symbols on their chests and speak in tongues.

Legislators of taste, famished after hours of sausage making, disrobe and disembowel an erudite economist. His formulas had to be savored before implementation.

A creature devoid of reason was excavated. Elders read entrails slowly spreading over the stone altar. They failed to comprehend the joy of the singing maiden.

Black and white photographs from the ongoing civil war alarmed the political prisoner. The stark contrast of evil and good emboldened his inquisitor. Torture continued after all pertinent information had been extracted. Superiors elevated her in the regime and the finest images from her interrogations are on display in the Temple of Art.

Seeds of eternity are spread through earthly desire.

Enraptured whores worship the flesh they void of spirit.

Essence of love streams endlessly into darkness. Silken dreams are spun in the womb of the Eternal Whore.

Wisdom resides in a freshly severed head.

Torture illuminates the inquisitor.

Stimulation of the brain clitoris agitates the unborn. They shriek in darkness until irruption.

Amputated hands caress pillars of Heaven. Thick ambrosia pools on tongues extended from severed heads. Eyes of solid amber are liquefied by ecstasy.

Pearlescent strings stretch slowly from the lips of a whore onto intestines strangling her. Semen from the Beast is the salvation of the world.

Mother, lover, offspring: pain amplifies desire for union with the Sacred Whore.

Soft creatures dissolve in a veil of tears. Follow the laughter of the Goat beyond this illusion.

The damned scream as they spiral upward. Truth incinerates incrustations of Spirit.

Shredding roses inebriates the Beast. Distended wombs of government discharge creatures of his imagination to ravish the body-politic.

Subjects do not choose how they live. The strong decide how lives are spent.

ABOUT THE AUTHOR

Duward was born and raised in Nome, Alaska. On frozen streets, under the Northern Lights, he walked with friends through the dark city. Laughter was more frequent as they aged. Drunk and stoned, they stumbled into stories you can hear on his Oral Delirium podcast. After years of excess he moved to Kentucky, where he currently resides.

www.ingramcontent.com/pod-product-compliance
Ingram Content Group UK Ltd.
Pitfield, Milton Keynes, MK11 3LW, UK
UKHW051133260726
13967UKWH00010B/3021